First published in the United States of America in 2003
by NVU Editions Wendy, LLC., 363 West Erie Street. 4W,
Chicago, IL 60610. nvuproductions.com

Designed by NVU Productions.
Distributed by NVU Editions Wendy, LLC.
Printed and bound in Italy.

ISBN 0-9724575-5-0

First Edition
1098765432

nesting

LIFESTYLE INSPIRATIONS FOR YOUR GROWING FAMILY

WENDY BELLISSIMO

written with Leslie Lehr Spirson

TO MY TIGERLILY AND BUTTERFLY, I LOVE AND ADORE YOU BOTH IN WAYS I NEVER IMAGINED POSSIBLE...TO THEIR NEW LITTLE SISTER, WHO HAS BEEN MY SWEET COMPANION THROUGH EVERY STAGE OF THIS BOOK...AND TO MY HUSBAND, A MAN OF STRENGTH AND CHARACTER, THE FATHER I ALWAYS DREAMED OF AS A LITTLE GIRL.

CONTENTS

nest•ing *vb*

1 : to build or occupy a nest

2 : to create and settle into a warm and secure refuge

www.websters.com

philosophy

Designing a beautiful nursery is like building the perfect nest. Choosing

colors and fabrics — or twigs and leaves — is only the beginning.

This special room is the backdrop of your child's earliest memories,

the heart of a whole new life. Already, your home is a reflection of

who you are, a combination of the twigs fallen from the sprawling

tree that has grown from the roots of your own experience. Now you

are expanding this environment to nurture your child, to create a

world made unique by the love you put into it. As you instinctively gather twigs to create a "warm and secure refuge" for your family, this book will encourage you to plant seeds as you go. So, fly beyond the treetops and venture into an enchanted forest of possibilities. Chapter by chapter, twig by twig, your dream will become a clear vision, and your vision will become a reality.

why nesting?

The world as you know it is about to change. As an expectant parent, you probably get that (or will get that) a lot. And if you're already a mother, you know exactly what those words mean — a new baby opens up a world of joy that, like a flavor you've never tasted, is impossible to imagine. From feeling the fuzz on caterpillars again for the first time, to finding bunnies in the clouds, and maybe even to cuddling up on a rainy day and watching "Teletubbies," I was looking forward to it all.

But then my friends, good intentioned as much as mischievous, had "briefed" me. With devilish grins only true veterans of babydom could manage they stood in the middle of my living room and told me to say "bye-bye" to it all — to pack it away for the next decade and brace myself.

At first, overwhelmed and hanging on every word of my new-mommy mentors, I was fine with this. And so looking forward to the heart-thumping joys of motherhood was I that I accepted the fact that some of the special touches which made my house a cozy home would have to go the way of my skinny jeans. But as time passed, something other than the baby was kicking at me from the inside.

The thing is, I am a designer. And that is not just a job description. At the age of seven, I was planning imaginary rooms with fabric swatches on the floor of my mother's Connecticut furniture store. My Barbies™ didn't care to frolic in the beach house with Ken™, because they were busy remodeling it. By sixteen I was happily making interior design calls to the homes of store customers, "de-shagging" the carpets and bringing classics back into the home. Today, I'm likely to dream up a whole new collection at the sight of a Jacaranda tree. The passion to create, enhance and transform has always defined my spirit and I decided that having a baby didn't mean having to put that aside. The new creation in my life would become the center, a center from which I would re-create my world, enhancing and transforming our lives in a way I had never imagined.

serendipity

I never specifically planned to become a designer for children; my career has sprung from serendipity as well as supply & demand. Growing up in my family's furniture store, I learned to appreciate both quality and craftsmanship. One year, when I found all of the popular school electives filled up, I learned how to sew. I was embarrassed by my new skill, right up until the assembly when I received the Home Ec Award — a particularly fine pair of scissors with my name engraved on them. I was destined for design school.

While studying in Holland, I was more impressed by the 2000-year-old cobblestone streets than the textbooks, so when the year was up, I slung on my backpack and traveled across the continent. Of course the art was amazing everywhere, but I was most impressed by how the Dutch use classic patterns in new and interesting ways, how the French use antiques along with their everyday utensils and how in Turkey, people sat on mismatched pillows of richly colored patterns and textures that combined to look incredible. An affinity for mixing it up while providing comfort, convenience and touchable elegance serves as the foundation of my style today.

a company is born

If the beginnings of my company could be called a birth then I guess you could say I got knocked up. I had no plans or intentions of having a business. It all started with basic necessity.

After moving to California and renting an apartment, all I could afford was a secondhand couch, a couch that was so funky I was afraid to sit down. Friends admired the slipcover and throw pillows I made so much that Joe (the guy who ultimately gave me this great name) suggested I sell them. I dug out my special scissors and the pile of discontinued fabrics I couldn't bear to throw away at the Malibu antique store where I worked, borrowed a sewing machine, and got to work. When Joe drove me to an upscale shopping area in Santa Monica, I went into the first boutique dragging two plastic bags stuffed with thirty pillows. They bought twenty-nine.

With the profit, I bought a thirty-year-old pea green sewing machine and started pounding the pavement — even while visiting my family in Connecticut.

A sale to a landmark New York City store gave me the confidence to try for the retailers gift show in San Francisco. I bought more fabric and sewed like mad. Then came the El Niño storm that flooded everything in our apartment. We camped with my new father-in-law, made a list of our losses, and gave up. We cancelled the rental van and hotel, and figured we'd eat the booth deposit. Then a funny thing happened: we woke up and the sun was shining. We decided to go for it.

A test order with Macy's and Nordstrom's got us a meeting with a larger retail chain, so I whipped up nine bedding sets, and sold all of them. Back in business, we struggled to find a loan, factory space, and enough people to complete the order in time. We did.

Two and a half years later, ten days before a big trade show in New York, I discovered a stockpile of yummy fabrics in my workroom that I hadn't been able to resist buying — fabrics that translated better to babies. On a whim, I spent the next seven nights creating crib linens, moses baskets and bassinets. The adult line had a solid base, but this was so much fun! It seemed like the sky was the only limit to my imagination. When I displayed my new products at the show — the most important show of the year — over half of our booth was filled with baby and children's linens! Uh-oh. I had no research, no marketing plan — I knew nothing about nursery products; I only knew what I liked. Fortunately, I didn't have much time to panic. When the doors opened, we were swamped with orders: Wendy Bellissimo baby 'n' kids was born.

Later I realized why the line was so well received. Most nursery products were based on the old standard of bright prints, with everything matching right down to the diaper stacker (a product I've never quite understood). With my design experience and my passion for mixing textiles, I saw fabrics with a different eye. Why not embroider a bunny on a sophisticated, but washable velvet? No one had ever seen crib bumpers with paneled slipcovers or bed skirts layered like petticoats. When people say my designs have influenced the overall look of baby bedding and nursery design they mean that the industry is no longer obsessed with infant-oriented patterns and primary colors. Now, the focus is on beauty.

Of course, you might have something special in mind for your baby. That's why I've worked really hard to provide you with the tools to design your own personal crib linens. While I have hundreds of magical combinations, the fabrics are interchangeable so you can follow your own inspiration. With Design Studio, software we developed solely to give parents a visual to work with, you can click a mouse and watch your bedding creation come to life. When I walk through the factory and see the amazing combinations that parents have designed themselves, I get so excited — I know that someone out there is going to be very happy.

My children have inspired me in so many ways. In life, they have given me more than I had ever dreamed of. As a bonus, they have made me better at what I do. Now, when I can't find something for them I make it myself. I've designed high chair pads, pacifier holders, clothing, accent rugs — even a beautiful sandbox. The line is ever expanding. Every day brings more ideas — if only it brought more time!

the new world

I sincerely wish I could be there with you to share the excitement of preparing for a new life. Since I can't, here are some of the things that I invariably tell my expectant friends (after resisting the temptation to scare the heck out of them with a devilish grin of my own!). Have confidence. Lay on the floor and imagine the room from your child's perspective, a room that will inspire your entire family. Think beyond the nursery. Other than for safety's sake, don't put up barriers. Never say "don't touch," either verbally or implied by your design. Instead, keep things within reach, and teach them how to interact with each and every item in your home. It takes decidedly more effort, but you will be amazed by how quickly they learn and how much easier this will make things for you in the long run. Remember that the coming years are a time of discovery, so be sure to give them a home in which they can discover. This will give them confidence. It will empower them. They will experience firsthand your trust, respect, and admiration — and that's what you'll get back from them. It begins at home…

It begins with nesting.

designing the nest

Have you ever noticed how no two nests are alike? Our feathered friends use twigs, leaves, and the occasional piece of yarn, but they each use different twigs and leaves — and sometimes the odd piece of tinsel. Eagles build for safety high up on cliffs and treetops; bowerbirds have been known to decorate only in shades of blue. So allow yourself to be enchanted with possibilities: designing the perfect nest is not just for the birds.

Parents often tell me that the nursery is the center of their universe long before the baby arrives. What could be more thrilling than imagining the first thing your child will see every morning or the last thing at night? Then again, what could be more overwhelming? Don't worry, here's where the fun begins. With a little planning, you can create a special place to snuggle up, a room as cozy as a hug.

a meaningful place

Remember when that baby was a mere twinkle in your eye? A wonderful nursery starts the same way: with a vision. When I was pregnant with Cecilia, I lay down on the bare floor and tried to imagine what this little corner of the world would look like to a newborn… or a crawler…or a toddler. It had to be magical from every angle, yet still accessible. I wanted to fill it with the kind of things that were special to me when I was young. But would the same things be special to her? Wouldn't she find her own favorites in a few years?

I decided to start with the basics and create a lasting environment. A place to dream and play, surrounded by soothing colors in soft muted shades. First, I needed a subtle theme. I love bunnies (my mom called me "bunny" when I was born), but I didn't want them breeding all over the place. It had to be meaningful, not mind-blowing. I decided to use bunnies as nuance, a sentimental motif that makes it clear she is part of me, part of us — that her room is a true family room.

Joe and I fell in love with the Tuscan countryside on an anniversary trip to trace our ancestral roots, so I decided to start there. Why not re-create this special place in a dreamy mural? Now we could all run through the hills together — past stone farmhouses and trees and animals — in our imaginations. It doesn't matter if you fill your walls with paint, wallpaper, or a border, as long as you keep it simple and soothing.

Color is the key to a magical mood. Cecilia's room had to incorporate the deep rich tones of our house, so I couldn't use anything too floral or overpowering. Soft green with a hint of petal pink bring to mind a spring flower blooming in a meadow. I love mixing sophisticated fabrics with a bit of whimsy, so here's where I added a personal touch: a little bunny that could have hopped right out of the countryside is embroidered onto the sage velvet panel of the creamy bumpers. Some of the same colors are used on the double crib skirt (sweetened by the beautiful sheer eyelet overlay) as well as the simple window treatments — but nothing too matchy. Cecilia's canopy crib continues the distinctive motif, while a mama and baby bunny have scampered clear across the room to her sturdy toy box.

Aside from the crib, I wanted the furniture to feel inviting for grown-ups as well as children. A comfy glider chair for nursing needs to be big enough for reading together later on — and the washable slipcover is perfect for when Gracie joins us with her big girl cup.

It's also important to create an art area, a place where your child is so comfortable she can get lost in her daydreams…and be truly inspired. A sturdy scaled-down table and chairs will do the trick, especially if it's adorned with your child's name. Be sure to make it personal, not perfect. Go ahead and pick up a paintbrush!

JOE AND I FELL IN LOVE WITH THE TUSCAN COUNTRYSIDE ON AN ANNIVERSARY TRIP TO TRACE OUR ANCESTRAL ROOTS, SO I DECIDED TO START THERE. WHY NOT RE-CREATE THIS SPECIAL PLACE IN A DREAMY MURAL?

THE DRAWERS IN CECILIA'S CHANGING TABLE HOLD DIAPER
NECESSITIES WHILE THE CUPBOARDS BENEATH PROVIDE TOY
STORAGE WITHIN HER REACH.

I believe in extended use for everything, both in design and construction. Instead of buying a changing table, you can attach a thick, slipcovered changing pad to a chest of drawers. Armoires are amazing for their space-saving capacity — plus you can keep toys on the bottom, at eye level and within reach for your child. It's a good way to keep clutter at a minimum. From the time Gracie and Cecilia were about seven months old, they liked to open and close the doors, so we've made it a game to put their toys away.

With all that banging, it's best to find furniture with a hand-rubbed or distressed finish. Not only does it look charming now, it will look just as good through years of nicks and scratches — so you can concentrate on your children's "ouchies," not the furniture's.

When we learned, by accident, that our second child was a girl, I designed the Bunny Love linens for extended use. Cecilia will have lots of time to get used to her big-girl bed — and, meanwhile, we'll all be comfortable spending time together in her room. I designed this bed with a delicately curved head- and sideboard that blends right in with the sloping hillside. The antique white finish adds an elegant and spacious feel to an area that could easily have looked crowded. By using the same sweet colors and soft fabrics in different combinations for the duvet cover, I avoided the busyness and repetition of a perfect match.

Wooden floors are not only beautiful, but the surface is great for toys. The rug, originally intended for adult use, grounds the room with timeless style. The powdery palette pulls all of the colors together, and will remain in the room long after the crib is gone.

Cecilia's bathroom was originally the guest bath, so I needed to add some whimsy to the natural slate and carved stone borders. Hand-painted gold stripes adorned with little green bunnies pick up on the colors and motif of Cecilia's room to make it uniquely hers.

HOW TO CREATE A DREAMY MURAL

- Use soft, muted tones.

- Keep animals small. Life-sized characters can be overwhelming.

- Put structures in the distance. Let your child imagine adventures on the way to the castle.

- Bring the picture to life with three-dimensional designs. Try a child-friendly wooden gate or sign that doubles as a coat rack.

THE GRACEFUL BED COVERED WITH SOPHISTICATED FABRICS HAS A TRUNDLE UNDERNEATH THAT IS SURE TO GET LOTS OF USE DURING SLEEPOVERS.

simple & sumptuous

Fabrics inspire me. I love mixing yummy textures: prints and chenilles, organdy and ginghams, toiles and velvets. A mixture adds extra interest to the room, and babies come to appreciate the tactile quality as they grow.

Kelly Ripa fell in love with the fairy-tale feel of Sir Leapsalot. Lavender is a fresh shade that adds a subtle feminine touch to the buttery yellow stripe and lime gingham fabrics.

A light blanket is more stylish than a quilt. This one, in soft white chenille, blends quietly with the woven gingham sheet. Rather than diluting the effect of Sir Leapsalot with yet another frog, I carried the dreamy mood onto the blanket with lavender stars.

The lilac embroidered organdy drapes and crib skirt add a touch of elegance and bring out the old world charm of the distressed white dresser. The sprightly changing pad on the top of the dresser reminds you to keep an eye on Sir Leapsalot as he bounds across a pillow to kiss the princess on the lavender chenille slipcovered chair.

Did I mention slipcovers? Putting the fun in functional, they are a must for both bumpers and chairs. Not only are they stylish and do they help the pillows maintain their shape, but they can be described by two of my favorite words: machine washable!

WHAT TO LOOK FOR:

- 100% natural fibers
- Machine washable
- Lightweight blanket
- Slipcovers
- Ties on corners, tops, bottoms, and centers of bumpers

WHAT TO CONSIDER WHEN DESIGNING A NURSERY:

- Choose a personal motif or subtle theme
- Select fabrics and colors
- Keep it soft & soothing
- Plan a functional layout
- Bangable furniture
- Closet and storage space
- Flooring
- Decorative touches

EMBROIDERED ORGANDY CURTAIN PANELS TOPPED WITH A BORDERED VALANCE ADD TO THE DREAMY EFFECT OF THE ROOM. THE GLIDER ROCKER SLIPCOVERED IN LAVENDER CHENILLE IS A COZY PLACE TO SNUGGLE UP.

KELLY RIPA FELL IN LOVE WITH MY SIR LEAPSALOT
DESIGN, WHICH WAS THE INSPIRATION FOR THE
FAIRY-TALE FEEL OF THE ROOM

babies will bloom

Flowers are a traditional favorite for girls, with their soft shapes and feminine colors. Too much of anything can be overwhelming — not to mention overstimulating to a child — so be careful not to overdo it, even with a delicate pattern like this.

Reserving the floral print for the featured position on the bumper, creams and soft greens highlight the curving leaves and round blossoms. Mixed with clean patterns such as stripes, pink never gets boring. In fact, these pale pink walls open up the room and keep the design from dominating the space.

While at first glance color may be the essence of this room, it's the way subtle motifs play off one another that makes the design work. The leaf detail on the elegant chandelier carries over the floral motif from the bedding and "baby love" art, while the custom covered shades bathe the room with a soft glow. The sheer eyelet trim on the sage green blanket blends with both the extravagant ruffle on the crib bumper and the simple panel of the window treatment to enhance the sweet yet sophisticated mood.

This adorable heart-shaped chaise lounge with its toile slipcover makes the perfect reading chair for a young lady, especially with the shelf at arm's reach. The bunnies hopping off the wall art onto the chaise keep things sentimental, while a touch of leopard on the pillow adds pizzazz for the hip modern babe.

FAR LEFT: RESERVING THE FLORAL PRINT FOR THE FEATURED POSITION ON THE BUMPER, CREAMS AND SOFT GREENS HIGHLIGHT THE CURVING LEAVES AND ROUND BLOSSOMS.

LEFT: THE CHILD-SIZED CHAISE LOUNGE WITH ITS TOILE SLIPCOVER ADDS ANOTHER TOUCH OF PLAYFUL SOPHISTICATION.

One of the easiest ways to change a nursery into a bedroom is to pick out things you truly love the first time around. Clean walls and simple window dressings flatter the evolution of any room. Basically, all I had to do to transform this nursery design into a big-girl room was remove the crib and pop a beautiful bed in its place.

A varied combination of the same fabric eases the transition. Too much of a good thing can be a bad thing, so rather than picking one main fabric for the duvet cover, the patch design incorporates the floral print while maintaining the understated elegance of the room. Of course, you may want to duplicate something that you really love and that really works, like the sage green velvet bed skirt trimmed in a pink ticking and sheer natural eyelet.

Bunnies on the iron bed frame keep things cozy. The old-fashioned figures aren't too fussy, and they make it clear that your growing girl will always be your baby.

While the pink ticking of the window treatments blended sweetly with the crib, now the sage green velvet stands out to highlight the bed linens. Lavish pillows complete the sumptuous look.

For a final touch, rearrange sentimental treasures to give them a new role. The plush bunny has earned a place of honor in the classic, hand-painted baby doll high chair. And with the chaise lounge tucked into a dreamy corner by the window, the former crib blanket will make a very special lap warmer.

WHEN CHANGING A NURSERY INTO A BEDROOM, YOU MAY WANT TO DUPLICATE SOMETHING THAT REALLY WORKS, LIKE THIS SAGE GREEN VELVET BED SKIRT TRIMMED IN A PINK TICKING AND SHEER NATURAL EYELET. A PILE OF PLUSH PILLOWS COMPLETE THE SUMPTUOUS LOOK WITHOUT BEING TOO PRECIOUS.

favorite things

Building a room around something you love is a wonderful way to begin designing your nursery. It can also be quite challenging — even if you're starting out with bare walls and a big budget. Mixing colors, textures, and time periods requires a theme that can encompass many moods. Country Walk was designed around Alex Kingston's vintage school room prints and linen windowpane drapes.

on the art, while the chenille and natural gingham crib sheet complement the draperies. Carrying these fabrics over to the changing table and glider chair adds continuity and warmth to the room.

From that point, furnishing choices were fairly simple: more soft natural colors with that vintage feel. A toile print mixed with denim customizes the padded toy box that doubles as a bench. My picnic style art table with the continuous roll of paper is the perfect focal point between the prints, softened by the "little door" bulletin / chalkboard set. Even the knickknack shelf topped by tulips that remind Alex of her native England adds to the schoolhouse mood. The classic beadboard bookcases are within easy reach from either side of the table.

I started where I always do, with the fabrics. We spent hours sitting on the concrete floor, combing through swatches to find the right combination of colors that would complement not only the prints, but the curtains as well. We wanted to pull a hint of pink from the pictures, but not so much as to be "girly girly," so I used the color as an accent to the simple yet highly textured fabrics of the bedding. The pink designer burlap, reversed denim, and mossy green velvet all picked up

Nature is the ideal complement to the schoolhouse, with a country scene that inspires a long "recess" on the wall behind the crib. The mural includes lots of personal touches for the baby to recognize, including the family dogs. This is especially appropriate, since the dogs love to hang out in this cozy room. My handmade leaf-adorned sconces reach out like branches from a painted tree. Daffodils brighten up the hillside.

I created the little lamb picture for the adjoining wall to draw the colors of the "schoolhouse" and the countryside together with a tender touch. A simple rug warms the floor between the hand-painted child-sized rocker and the family rocker.

As long as the basic design is simple, you can carry the accent colors right down to the dresser drawer knobs.

sentimental touches

Just because you know the sex of your baby, doesn't mean you have to design your nursery around the news. Catherine Bell knew she was having a baby girl, but she was more interested in making the room personal than she was in making it overtly feminine.

When Catherine was young, her mother called her "Mooshy" (for mouse), so I designed the embroidered mama and baby mouse on the crib bumpers to reflect this sentimental nickname. When the grandma-to-be came to see the nursery for the first time and saw "Mooshy" on the decorative pillow, tears came to her eyes.

The mural is just as meaningful. Catherine showed me pictures of a vacation she and her husband had taken to Northern Italy, so I designed a scene that featured both their favorite view and their favorite villa. The highlight of the trip was the day they indulged in a favorite hobby, motorcycle racing, at the famed Ducati racetrack. The little motorcycle racing through the hills above the art table is sure to inspire wonderful stories and imaginative art.

The soft sherbet and greens of the mural carry over to the crib linens and slipcovered glider rocker to keep the mood airy and light. The tailored lines of the crib linens and the solid colored fabrics allow you to focus on the sentimental touches.

THE SLIPCOVERS ON THESE LIGHTWEIGHT OTTOMANS ARE EMBROIDERED WITH THE ENDEARING MESSAGES "PLAY WITH ME" AND "CREATE WITH ME." THESE ARE EASILY MOVED AROUND THE ROOM FOR MOM AND DAD OR ANY VISITOR WHO WANTS TO JOIN IN ON THE FUN.

THE MAMA AND BABY MOUSE EMBROIDERY WAS INSPIRED
BY CATHERINE'S CHILDHOOD MEMORIES OF HER MOM CALLING
HER "MOOSHY" (FOR MOUSE).

at home in the hills

The rich colors of the Indigo Star design give this little rider a rugged place to grow in a small town where bridle paths line every road. To personalize the nursery addition for this family's third child, we decided to blend fabulous fabrics with deep wood tones. The mural that depicts frolicking ponies and a baby foal nuzzling with his mama give the room such an open-air feeling that you can imagine the sweet smell of hay.

Plaid makes an amazing accent when it's bordered with dark solids on the nine patch blanket and goes solo on the changing pad across the room. A rustic green diaper box sits conveniently beside it. An extra blanket with vintage biplanes hangs from a hook on the side, ready to warm a lap on those cold country nights. It also brings out the deep forest green of the glider rocker and adds to the boyish mood.

Ryan's art table has country-style spindle legs distressed to look like he's already had his spurs on it, so the next scratch won't be any big deal. The bulletin board with matching frame adds height to the low corner and is positioned so that Ryan's art is lit by streams of sunshine coming in the window. The child-sized chairs are painted to pick up the barn red of the carpet that lays on the rough hewn hardwood floors.

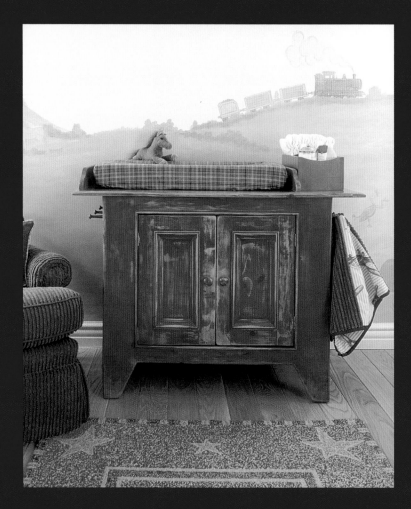

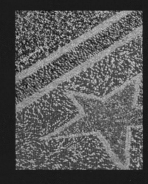

THIS NURSERY WILL TRANSFORM EASILY INTO A BIG-BOY ROOM BY REPLACING THE CRIB WITH A TWIN BED COVERED IN THE SAME HANDSOME FABRICS THAT COMPLEMENT THE WINDOW VALANCES, AREA RUG, AND GLIDER ROCKER.

With the distinctive ponies prancing 'round the iron canopy, there was no need for a stampede. Instead, I designed the Buck Star rug to coordinate with the stars that brand the pillow on the slipcovered chair. The simple shape extends to delicate baby-sized stars on the charcoal gingham bumpers and valances.

My favorite part of this mural is the personalized sign with a real plank of wood that comes to life as a coat rack. I designed two jackets with some of the same fabrics used in the bedding, both handy and handsome.

Deep red adds a tender touch to the moses basket as well as the elegant valances. Decorative touches are clean and simple, like the wooden rocking horse and the occasional stuffed pony. The handy wagon, with its red rails, is a cute way to keep clutter off the floor.

life's little surprises

Even if the gender of your baby is a mystery, your nursery design doesn't have to be. Once the surprise is revealed, you'll be far too busy to decorate. A warm buttery yellow is one way to go — but it's not the only way.

Country singer Sara Evans didn't know if she was having a boy or a girl, but she knew what she liked when she saw this Farmers Party print. The colors of brick, gold, and sage in ginghams and stars provide lots of interest and are ideal accent colors for this unisex fabric. They let the playful animals pop without having to risk overdoing the fun print.

All of the wooden furniture was hand-painted to complement the design. I also created all of the artwork in the room to bring out the whimsical figures of the Farmers Party. I love how the natural chenille borders the crib skirt and adds extra texture while the star pattern on the bumpers and blanket give the design a dreamy feel.

WHETHER A BOY OR A GIRL, THIS BABY WILL BE ENTERTAINED BY A MUSICAL PARADE OF FROGS, BEARS, BUNNIES, AND MONKEYS ON THE CENTER PANEL OF THIS CRIB BUMPER.

AN ARMOIRE WITH EXTRA STORAGE SPACE IS ADORNED WITH SUBTLE CHARACTERS THAT ADD TO THE PLAYFUL MOOD OF THE ROOM.

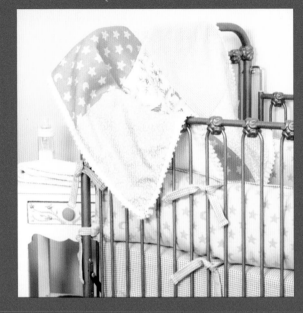

THE SAGE STAR SLIPCOVER ON THE
GLIDER ROCKER PROVIDES THE PERFECT
BALANCE FOR THE CHANGING TABLE ON
THE OPPOSITE SIDE OF THE ROOM.

I DESIGNED THE ABC 123
ARTWORK TO COMPLEMENT
THE FARMER'S PARTY
FABRIC AS WELL AS TO
INSPIRE LEARNING

love

bee happy

Bee Happy is a friendly unisex design that can be used over and over as your family grows. The embroidered bees on the inner bumper panels offer great stimulation for baby, while the green, yellow, and white palette provides a sunny combination of warm and cool tones. You can personalize the simple theme by adding things that reflect your little one's personality as time goes on.

The Bee Happy art creates a lively mood and sets off the black and white gingham trim on the bumpers and chenille rocker slipcover. And who can resist this baby bee buzzing around the moses basket?

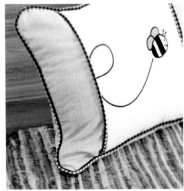

SPENCER

SIMON

two's company

Twins are twice as much to love, but don't need twice as much space. While Lisa Anne Walters' boys appear quite happy to sleep in the drawers of this classic double dresser with a changing table top, they'll find plenty of room to stretch out in this cozy nursery. The calming colors of the Lemon Drop Collection opens up the space. The boys will soon develop their own individual styles, but for now it's best to begin with simple, identical bedding. Let the personalities be the standouts from the start.

Solid colors on delicious textures are the key to clean simplicity — the busiest pattern is a pale blue stripe. Patchwork blankets pick up the colors of the linens with a fresh, sunny feel. The dreamiest touch is the sheer star layered over the citrus colored bedskirts.

For the cribs, we chose a classic spindle design that adds to the "retro" feel of the nursery rhyme figures Lisa had already painted as a chair rail. To add an extra airy feeling to the space, we brushed a thin coat of whitewash over the chair rail and applied pale green to the lower walls.

Decorative touches should be simple as well — note the pale yellow chenille of the changing pad and the crisp white slipcover on the glider in front of the window. A throw pillow adds that special touch, especially with the same sheer star that is layered over the bedskirt. Hand-painted name signs in coordinating colors pull everything together — and remind visitors who's who.

love grows here

The Sedaka twins' nursery is warmed by the enchantment of the Love Grows Here embroidery. While the walls are dressed with swaying trees and white ponies, the room remains soothing and calm, thanks to the focal point of simple but luxurious linens.

Antiqued cribs dressed in pleasing fabrics anchor both sides of the large window. Soft light streams through blush colored Roman shades.

Ah, to sit and dream on a slipcovered window seat. Fluffy pillows with extravagantly long ruffled edges add the feminine touch to what is otherwise a simple but sophisticated look. The cut velvet of the bed skirt also adorns the shades of the elegant reading sconces on each end of the alcove. This window seat has the dual purpose of providing a lounging area as well as a storage area camouflaged by wide deep drawers.

The armoire also has a secret function — the top doors open to the diaper changing area. Picnic baskets that look as if they could be carried right into the relaxing mural scene (that continues inside the armoire) hang conveniently on the doors to keep diapers and essentials handy. We left the garment rod in the armoire for when the twins graduate from diapers and need the space for hanging clothes.

The sweet moses basket resting on the wooden stand can be moved about the house with ease, allowing you to take a beautiful part of the nursery along wherever you go.

PICNIC BASKETS THAT LOOK AS IF THEY COULD BE CARRIED RIGHT INTO THE RELAXING
MURAL SCENE (THAT CONTINUES INSIDE THE ARMOIRE) HANG CONVENIENTLY ON THE
DOORS TO KEEP DIAPERS AND ESSENTIALS HANDY.

A CHILD-SIZED ART TABLE RESTS AMONG
THE LILY PADS, ALL SET WITH TEA FOR TWO.
WE EXTENDED THE WALL BETWEEN THE
ENTRY DOOR AND CLOSET JUST ENOUGH
TO ACCOMMODATE THIS PLAY AREA.

THE MOST LUXURIOUS FABRICS CAN STILL BE MACHINE
WASHABLE. HERE, LINENS, COTTONS, BELGIAN VELVETS,
AND CUT VELVETS WILL STAND UP TO THE TWINS AS WELL
AS TO THE FAMILY DOGS, WHO'VE MADE THIS WINDOW
SEAT THEIR NEW HOME.

big challenges

Transforming a large space with soaring ceilings and wide white walls may seem like a wonderful problem, but when the goal is creating a cozy space for a tiny new life, it takes a great deal of planning and imagination to solve.

Since a child is disproportionately small in any room, an abundance of fabrics and details can be overwhelming. Simplicity is the key to keeping the colors flowing and to encompass the room in both warmth and energy. Also, be sure to keep tables, toys, and decorative touches at a low, child-friendly level.

First, the fun part: fabric. Just as we keep smaller rooms light to create an optical illusion of space, here's an excuse to use deeper, richer shades of the same calming colors. Plush fabrics such as velvet can be combined in slightly bolder than usual combinations — as long as they are complemented by gentle neutrals, like this soothing vanilla velvet. Any prince

or princess might imagine riding the white stallion towards the castle, yet the storybook feel of the distant structure keeps things gentle enough for a baby.

The four-poster crib fills this space beautifully, allowing the imagination to soar along with the gilded birds resting on the posts.

Many newer homes with high ceilings have equally high windows. Use window treatments to warm the room. The chandelier adds the perfect medieval touch and helps to bring the ceiling level down.

The child-sized slipcovered rocker is my favorite piece in the room. It's easy to envision this little dreamer grabbing a favorite book or stuffed animal from the lined goody basket and nestling in.

The art table in this room is a warm round shape enhanced by the same silvery blue of the waterfall.

growing by leaps and bounds

How many nights will you spend listening for every burp and sigh from your new baby? Once out of the bassinet, the crib can feel awfully far away. One solution is to keep a twin bed handy.

By remaining true to your vision and extending the design from the crib to the bed linens, the room can be a welcome resting place for everyone in the family. Later, with the big-kid bed already in place, your child's transition from the crib will be a smooth one. Especially if a new baby will soon take up residence.

Teri Polo loves frogs. When she saw Sir Leapsalot she knew exactly what she wanted — the crowned prince and the rest of the royal family. Beginning with the same soft green base, I gave this collection a masculine spin by adding strong colors, including blues and reds. By using soft naturals in place of the crisp whites of Kelly Ripa's version of Sir Leapsalot, I've created a relaxing mood fit for a King.

A hint of red chenille on the bumper carries over to the bed skirt and duvet cover on the big-boy bed. The onyx check on the changing pad adds to the picnic theme while providing contrast to the hand-painted changing table. The bark-colored faux suede on the pillow sham anchors the bed into the frog pond mural on the wall.

Special details in this room include the little antique gold crowns custom-made to "crown" the crib posts. My favorite part of this room is the real wooden door of the "Frog Pad" that swings open from the wall to reveal Sir Leapsalot himself. I can just picture a child opening and shutting the door, giggling all the while.

THE ONYX CHECK CHANGING PAD COVER ADDS THE PERFECT CONTRAST TO THIS DRESSER AND HIGHLIGHTS THE PICNIC THEME PAINTED JUST ABOVE.

I CAN JUST PICTURE A CHILD OPENING AND SHUTTING THE DOOR, GIGGLING ALL THE WHILE.

I GAVE THIS COLLECTION A MASCULINE SPIN BY ADDING STRONG COLORS, INCLUDING BLUES AND REDS. A HINT OF THE RED CHENILLE ON THE BUMPER CARRIES OVER TO THE BED SKIRT AND DUVET COVER. THE DEEP, SOLID COLORS ON THE DUVET COVER MAKE THE TWIN BED APPEALING FOR A GROWING BOY.

my first nursery

Designing a nursery for my first child was such a thrill — here was my chance to create a unique and inspiring environment for my own family, a way to welcome our baby to a home full of love.

I admit, there was a lot of pressure! Store owners kept calling to see what I was going to do. Since we didn't know if we were having a boy or a girl, all I knew was that it had to be a unisex design. Now, it was my turn to answer the important questions that I ask other parents.

Since the room that would become the nursery is near our living room, a "great room" with rich bronzy patterns on the slipcovered sofas and an eclectic mix of dark wood, I decided to make the room an extension of both our style and the grassy yard outside the French doors. I stretched out on the hard wood floor and imagined our baby resting in the crib, staring out at the blue sky. I imagined this child hard at work on a drawing or playing dress-up with a friend. I wanted to surprise our baby with special touches, like a bunny peeking out from behind the armoire and our family dogs flying a biplane across the skylight soffit or flying in a beautiful hot air balloon. I wanted to create a soft, safe world with no limits.

OUR FAMILY DOGS GLIDE ACROSS THE SKY IN THE MAGICAL HOT AIR BALLOON AND PILOT THIS BIPLANE ACROSS GRACIE'S SKYLIGHT SOFFIT.

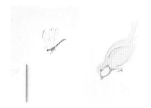

So I created Sweet Cricket, a sky full of sheer stars, patterned over denim, combined with a meadow of green gingham. The words *sweet - dreams - baby - love* are embroidered, one on the center of each bumper, to create a personal message for our new bundle of joy.

The antique gold crib is topped with stars that appear to float in the sky so the baby can gaze up and make a wish. To save space, I installed a changing pad, handy diaper boxes, and an interesting mobile inside the hand-painted distressed armoire. The bottom section serves as the perfect place to keep toys within a child's reach — and the perfect place to tuck them away.

Since Joe and I wanted more children, I decided to create an inviting space for future siblings to share. Planning ahead, I designed this bunk in a bump-able hand-rubbed green that looks like it sprouted from the meadow on the wall mural.

When Gracie Mae was born, I could easily have added some feminine flourishes, but the design worked — and it still works today. The bunk bed linens are classic Americana colors that my children will feel comfortable with at any age. Gracie's bunk bed turned out to be a good decision; at two years, she was already sleeping on the cozy bottom bunk.

Gracie's art area is snuggled in an alcove where her bulletin/chalkboard is designed to look like a little country house. Her name on the distressed denim blue chairs makes it clear that this is Gracie's territory. I made sure the small chairs had no arms, so big people can join her here, too.

When Gracie began to crawl, she'd stop and smile at the painted bunny, turtle, and frog. Now she calls them by name. Seeing how these little things touch her makes me feel really good about what I do for a living.

GRACIE'S BUNK BED TURNED OUT TO BE A GOOD CHOICE; AT TWO YEARS, SHE WAS ALREADY SLEEPING ON THE COZY BOTTOM BUNK. TO ADD SPACE I TRANSFORMED THE TOP SECTION OF THIS ARMOIRE INTO A CHANGING STATION. THE BOTTOM SECTION SERVES AS THE PERFECT PLACE TO KEEP TOYS WITHIN A CHILD'S REACH — AND THE PERFECT PLACE TO TUCK THEM AWAY.

ready *four* anything

When you start with clean classic lines, redecorating is a snap. Here, I've created two unisex looks and two gender specific looks from the Wendy Bee™ line simply by changing the fabrics.

This neutral background of pale green provides a dazzling display of versatility. The basics are simple: a traditional crib, a pale green changing table with straw baskets to hold diapers, and a natural weave rug on the hardwood floor. Now see what an amazing difference you can make with your choice of color and a personal motif. Abracadabra....

BOY'S ROOM This firehouse room looks custom made for a baby boy, especially with the fire engine embroidered on the center of the bumper between panels of soft blue. The red touches add a vibrant splash of color without overwhelming the look. An adorable retro version of the firehouse dalmatian is embroidered on the blanket corner. The seagrass check crib sheet blends with the background wall and extends to the decorative pillow. The complementary fabrics and fire engine red trim pull the room together with style. Natural chenille lightens the look as it is carried over to the slipcovered glider. As a final touch, I combined the soft blue and the sea grass check for the paneled curtains.

GIRL'S ROOM Anyone looking for the former little boy's room would clear out of this nursery in a hurry. The sweet Flutterby design highlighted by butterfly embroidery on the center bumper panels clearly indicate girl territory. White terry velour adds soft texture to the rest of the bumper. While apple green and white gingham picks up on the wall color and provides a crisp, neutral accent, the sheer star drapes and snowy white chenille add a dreamy touch.

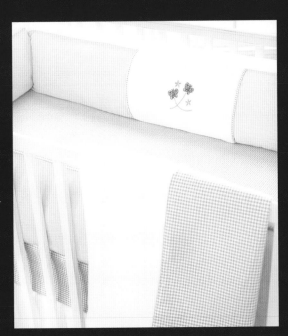

UNISEX Babies love farm animals, so this design is a hit with both boys and girls. The combination of antique gold and brick warms up the pale green walls like the early morning sun in a sweeping pasture. The embroidered horse, cow, pig, and sheep grazing on the center bumper panels will make every baby smile. My antique gold star fabric adds magic and warmth to the bumper and blanket. The brick and natural check of the crib sheet expands the farmhouse theme and melts softly into the natural terry velour trimmed crib skirt. Sheer star drapes resemble the country sky and draw attention to the same overlay on the decorative pillow.

UNISEX The Hoppily Ever After design is a cheerful way to make boys and girls feel at home in their royal kingdom. Prince and Princess frogs greet the baby from the center bumper panels, surrounded by sunshine yellow terry velour. Here, the clean, crisp yellow against the apple green and white check crib sheet create a sprightly mood. The soft fabrics, extended to the blanket, keep things restful. White chenille on the rocker shows off the pillow that pulls the look together with yellow terry panels bordering the sheer star overlay on the apple gingham. The star pattern on the sheer drapes adds to the enchantment.

fun with paints

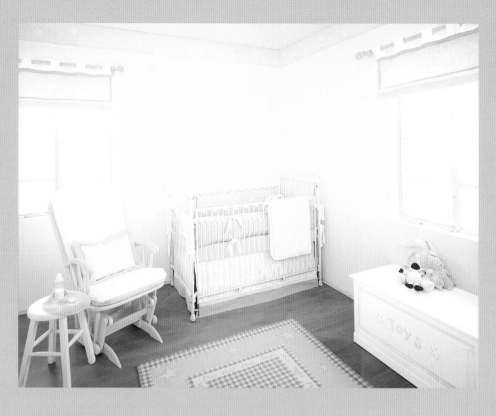

To create this colorful nursery, we got crafty with paints. The expectant parents knew they were having a boy, but wanted to keep a unisex design for the room in case their next baby would be a girl. After selecting the Starlight crib linens and area rug, we purchased primer, paint, tape, and stencils. Now we were ready to have some fun. I started with my own mixture of pale yellow for the walls and added a soft border of stars with a sponge stamp.

Next came the floors. After exposing the raw wood with a rented sander, the diamond pattern of a light and dark green hue was created to pick up on the lime gingham fabric accents.

We expanded the design by painting unfinished pieces of furniture. The changing table was the most exciting, decorated to create a nice balance with the crib. Fresh stripes of yellow and white are accented with green drawer pulls which carry the star motif over from the area rug and wall border. The toy chest makes its mark with a simple stencil and more colorful paints.

THE INSPIRATION FOR THIS NURSERY CAME FROM THE CRIB LINENS AND AREA RUG. THE PARENTS KNEW THEY WERE HAVING A BOY, BUT WANTED TO BE SURE THAT IF A GIRL CAME NEXT, THIS ROOM WOULD BE APPROPRIATE FOR HER, TOO.

HAND PAINTING THIS CHANGING
TABLE PROVIDED A UNIQUE AND
BEAUTIFUL BALANCE WITH THE
CRIB. WHEN DIAPERS ARE NO LONGER
NEEDED, JUST POP THE TOP OFF AND
YOU'LL HAVE A TRADITIONAL DRESSER.

WITH A RENTED FLOOR SANDER AND
PAINTERS TAPE, YOU CAN CREATE A SEA
OF DIAMONDS ON YOUR FLOOR.

one for all

Changing a boy's room into a girl's room may seem daunting, but even a tricky transition like this can be accomplished with ease. Whether you need a unisex room for the first baby, or you want to plan ahead for the last, remember: heaven is in the details.

Painting broad baby blue stripes may seem more appropriate for a little boy, but it can be just as lovely for a girl. Beginning with pale shades of pastels is always a good idea for a nursery and here, the masculine touch is found in the safari theme.

BOY From the creamy iron canopy where wild animals rule, to the mama and baby (or papa and baby) giraffes and elephants on the slipcovered velvet bumpers, your baby will be filled with wonder. A muted leopard print sheet adds to the safari feel, especially with floor length curtains to match. Baby blue on the bed skirt and the bumper slipcovers brings out the stripes on the walls. The green ticking on the slipcovered chair coordinates with the bottom of the bed skirt and bumper ties. In addition to a personal touch, the sturdy initials on the wall extend a jungle green detail picked up on pillows and wall art.

CREATING A SAFARI THEME DOESN'T HAVE TO RESULT IN A DARK, OVERWHELMING JUNGLE. HERE, I'VE CREATED A LIGHT AND CALMING PALETTE THAT BOTH SOOTHES AND INSPIRES.

TO GIRL When a little girl moves into this room, you don't have to change the walls. These crib linens incorporate the baby blue while adding the shades of pink and yellow that make it clear that this time, it's a girl. Tiny flowers embroidered on the ruffled slipcovered bumpers are an extra special touch.

Next, I changed the curtains to a sheer organdy drape with tiny daisies, the same fabric used over blue on the nine patch blanket and on the bumper panel.

Keep in mind that you don't have to go all out with the pink. The pale yellow blends with the wall and is just as soothing. This loveseat, slipcovered in the same buttercup stripe as the inner crib bumper, creates a reading area that a little girl can cuddle up in and call her own.

The adorable winged ballerina bunny makes a huge statement with very little space — and her blue tutu makes the walls the perfect backdrop for her dance. The vertical bookshelf designed to look like a doll house with a cottage style roof and shutters is a practical way to add magic to a little girl's room.

THIS ADORABLE WINGED BALLERINA BUNNY MAKES A HUGE STATEMENT WITH VERY LITTLE SPACE.

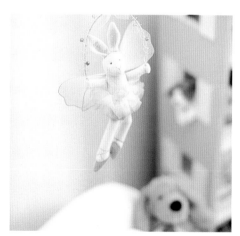

TO UNISEX Taking these same blue and cream striped walls to a unisex look can be made simple by choosing classic fabrics and furniture.

This delicate toile pattern in deep blue would please any baby boy or girl. The words "baby" and "love" embroidered in sage green on the center bumper panels are framed by coordinating velvet piping. White eyelet borders the green toile crib skirt and carries over to the curtain, a simple drape of sheer white eyelet topped with the green toile as a valance. The traditional charm of the cherry sleigh style crib adds warmth to the room.

Soft green accents are picked up in decorative touches, first in the "Cow Jumped Over the Moon" art, and finally on the hand-painted rocker. The moses basket, with its cozy white chenille patch blanket, is accented by an embroidered baby lamb.

Once the baby is born, you can personalize the room with an added touch of color, perhaps a stuffed pink piglet for a girl or blue corduroy cow for a boy.

"THE COW JUMPED OVER THE MOON" ARTWORK MAKES A SWEET STATEMENT THAT HELPS TO PULL THE ENTIRE LOOK TOGETHER.

THIS ROOM OFFERS A TIMELESS, TRADITIONAL ELEGANCE FOR A BABY BOY OR GIRL.

ready, set, grow

When Sara Evans needed a nursery for her second baby, we felt it was also time for her three-year-old son, Avery, to get a big-boy room. Luggage stripes, ginghams, solids, and chenilles will suit Avery even after he's outgrown his love for trains —— like the one I embroidered on his pillow.

I found this leather trunk to use as a bedside chest and hand painted the star on it to tie in the pillow sham and the rug. I even spray painted gold stars to a rugged brown color, then glued them on a burlap lamp shade. All of these little touches add character to the room. Avery thinks it's the bunk bed that makes the space magical, and summons all family visitors to his room so he can show it off.

The handy round ottoman, with its luggage stripe slipcover, makes a comfy seat for Avery or a grown-up visitor. It also creates a nice balance with the Roman window shade on the other side of the room.

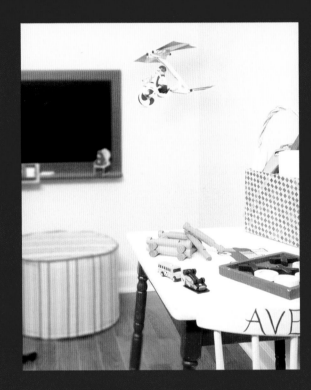

IT'S EASY TO PERSONALIZE AND ADD CHARACTER TO YOUR CHILD'S ROOM. HERE, I ADDED RUGGED STARS TO THIS BURLAP LAMPSHADE. WHAT'S NEEDED: SPRAY PAINT, A HOT GLUE GUN, AND ABOUT TWENTY MINUTES.

feathering the nest

Birds fly high and low searching for soft materials to line their nests. Some mama birds pamper their young with feathers plucked from their very own breasts. Fortunately, we can provide a warm homecoming simply by planning ahead. Although it's hard to imagine that such a tiny person could need so many things, you'll have fun preparing all the little details that feather the nest. When this task is completed, you can sit back and dream about swaddling your precious baby in a blanket and holding him 'til your heart's content.

moses basket

The moses basket is — hands down — the shower gift that gets the most enthusiastic response after it's actually used. When the gift is opened, it's mainly appreciated for its aesthetics. But when the newborn baby comes home and settles into family life, the moses basket becomes the workhorse, hero of the first three months.

At night, you can place the moses basket in bed between you and your partner, keeping the baby close without worrying about rolling over in your sleep. In the bathroom, it provides a safe haven while you take a quick shower. The moses basket is handy in the crib for afternoon naps and moves about the house easily.

I found that these cozy little baskets made it easy for our babies to learn to sleep contentedly on their own. They were close enough for me to attend to every whimper, but still safe in their own space. When it's time to graduate to the bassinet or crib, the baby is already accustomed to these surroundings, making the transition smoother.

Moses baskets go anywhere, like a portable nest. If you get one as a gift, give that friend a big hug!

bassinet

The dream goes something like this: You swaddle your sweet little baby and bring her home to the beautiful nursery. Sleepy-time comes and you lay her in the dreamy crib, creep to the door and close it quietly, smiling as you leave. Well, good luck. The reality is, for the first few months, you are going to want your little one by your side at every moment for security and comfort. A bassinet is an excellent way to accomplish that.

Some rock, some roll on wheels, some even have sheer "trains" cascading from their hoods to keep the critters away. Whichever you choose, your bassinet will become a practical family heirloom. Gracie slept in her "natural bee" bassinet for five months before we set it aside for her sister. Both reacted the same way to the little embroidered bee on the liner: first staring at it, then reaching for it, then babbling to it. They kicked their arms and legs, giddy with delight whenever we pulled the sheer star netting over the top. It was perfect for keeping them close by at night, while still allowing them their own sleeping space (especially once they had outgrown their moses baskets). Our bassinet was the setting for many touching memories — I am looking forward to making new ones with our next bundle of joy.

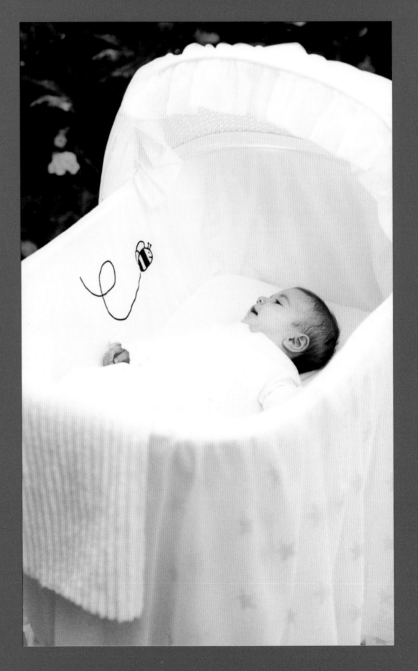

layette

A layette is the basic set of essentials that your newborn will need, day in and day out. Although most items get their fair share of use in the first twelve weeks, many of these standards will take on new uses as your little one continues to grow.

Don't wait for your baby shower to plan your layette. Friends love to give fancy frocks — usually too fancy for everyday use. If you already love to shop, you are in for a treat: buying basics for your precious baby's homecoming can be the most thrilling shopping experience of your life.

A newborn's clothing should be soft and simple, made from 100% cotton to protect the baby's tender skin. Test the fabric by rubbing it gently across the thin skin inside your wrist. It should feel nothing short of velvety soft. Flannel is much softer than terry or plain cotton when it comes to both wash and burp cloths. I like white everything, not only because it works for both sexes, but also because it looks so fresh and timeless. The number of items you purchase depends on how often you plan to wash them. Choose tee shirts that have a snap or tie-side so that you don't have to pull them over the baby's head. Long-sleeve tee shirts should have built-in hand mitts to protect your baby from scratching that sweet face. Also, save the snug one-piece snap bottom tops until after the umbilical cord has fallen off.

Gowns are best, but be sure they snap all the way down the front. This way, you can avoid pulling it over baby's head plus have easy access for diaper changes. A drawstring ribbon at the bottom will help keep the baby cozy.

Gracie and Cecilia wore their newborn essentials (pictured on the next page) so consistently that we affectionately named it "the uniform." This is the easiest set of basics for mom and dad and the most comfy for any newborn. There is simply no fussing here. (Remember to pre-wash all of your baby's clothing with a mild baby detergent.)

HAND MITTS
RECEIVING BLANKETS

FLANNEL SWADDLE BLANKETS

FULL SNAP-FRONT GOWN
HAT

SNAP-SIDE TEE
BOOTIES

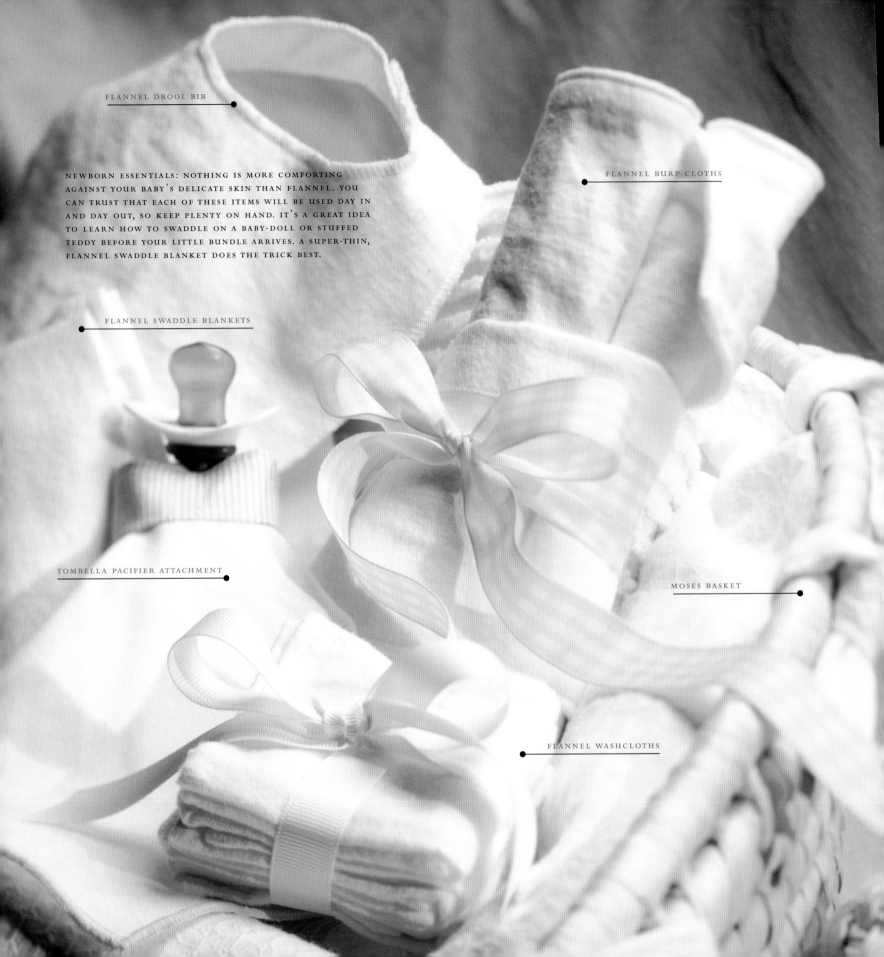

FLANNEL DROOL BIB

FLANNEL BURP CLOTHS

NEWBORN ESSENTIALS: NOTHING IS MORE COMFORTING AGAINST YOUR BABY'S DELICATE SKIN THAN FLANNEL. YOU CAN TRUST THAT EACH OF THESE ITEMS WILL BE USED DAY IN AND DAY OUT, SO KEEP PLENTY ON HAND. IT'S A GREAT IDEA TO LEARN HOW TO SWADDLE ON A BABY-DOLL OR STUFFED TEDDY BEFORE YOUR LITTLE BUNDLE ARRIVES. A SUPER-THIN, FLANNEL SWADDLE BLANKET DOES THE TRICK BEST.

FLANNEL SWADDLE BLANKETS

TOMBELLA PACIFIER ATTACHMENT

MOSES BASKET

FLANNEL WASHCLOTHS

SNAP-SIDE TEE AND PANT.   TIE-SIDE TEE AND PANT.   TIE-SIDE, SNAP-BOTTOM SHIRT.

the basics

The "uniform" is just the beginning of what you will need for your baby's first wardrobe. You will need other basics as well, including pant outfits for when you're on the go so that you can buckle your baby into a car seat properly. Keep in mind that extra comfort for baby usually makes things more convenient and functional for mom and dad. Be sure that all items are made of velvety-soft cotton, even if it's just the simplest tee shirt. Items that have snap or tie sides are a number one choice for me because most babies don't like clothing pulled over their heads. And with newborns, between diapers and spit-up, changes are necessary again and again in just one day.

Layette list Keep in mind that quantities depend on how often you plan on doing laundry; styles depend on the season in which your baby is born. For sizing, newborn and up to three months are usually the best choices. Cecilia was so big that she started with mostly three-month sizes and quickly graduated to six months. Here is a handy guideline for the ideal layette list:

- 4–6 full snap-front gowns with drawstring bottom
- 4–6 short-sleeve snap or tie-side tees
- 2–4 long-sleeve snap or tie-side tees with built-in hand mitts
- 4–8 tie-side snap-bottom shirts — long and short sleeves
- 2–4 lap-shoulder snap-bottom shirts — long and short sleeves
- 4–6 pull-on elastic waist pants
- 2–4 diaper covers
- 2 button-down sweaters
- 1 bunting
- 1 coming home outfit
- 4 pair of hand mitts
- 4 simple cotton hats
- 6 pair of socks
- 2 pair of moccasin socks
- 3 pair of booties
- 1 pair of crib shoes
- 4-6 swaddle blankets
- 4 receiving blankets
- 2 stroller blankets
- 6–8 flannel drool bibs
- 12 flannel burp cloths
- 12 flannel washcloths
- 3 hooded bath towels
- 4 terry washcloths
- 4 Tombella™ pacifier attachments
- 2 small soft rattles
- 1 moses basket with extra sheet
- 1 bassinet with extra sheet
- Christening, baby naming, or bris ceremony outfit
- After-ceremony attire: beautiful, comfy outfit (see page 80)

COMING HOME OUTFIT: GRACIE AND CECILIA BOTH WORE THIS SOFT KNITTED OUTFIT FOR THEIR HOMECOMING. TO SAY "IT'S A GIRL" I WRAPPED THEM IN A SIMPLE, PINK CHENILLE RECEIVING BLANKET. OUR NEXT LITTLE BLESSING WILL SHARE THIS SAME COMING HOME SWEATER SET.

1

A SOFT COTTON KNIT
SWEATER WITH SWEET
ELEPHANT BUTTONS WILL
SUIT A BABY BOY OR A
BABY GIRL.

2

THIS LAP-SHOULDER
SNAP-BOTTOM TEE IS
BEAUTIFULLY TRIMMED
IN SOFT PINK OR BABY
BLUE AND CAN BE PAIRED
WITH COZY PULL-ON
COTTON PANTS. IN WARMER
WEATHER, PAIR IT WITH
A CUTE DIAPER COVER.

3

CRIB SHOES ARE HARD
TO RESIST BECAUSE THEY
ARE SO CUTE. SINCE
THEY ARE FOR SPECIAL
OCCASIONS, ONE PAIR
FOR YOUR NEWBORN
SHOULD DO JUST FINE.

4

THE SOFT, ELONGATED
NECK ON THIS LITTLE
GIRAFFE IS THE PERFECT
SIZE FOR A NEWBORN'S
TINY HANDS TO GRASP.
THEY LOVE TO HOLD ON
TIGHT TO THINGS BUT
MOST SOFT RATTLES ARE
TOO BIG. ALTHOUGH
HARD RATTLES USUALLY
HAVE A SMALL GRASPING
POINT, NEWBORNS ARE
LIKELY TO BONK THEM-
SELVES IN THE HEAD.

something special

After a christening, baby naming or bris, you'll want to put your baby into a more comfy outfit, but one that's beautiful enough for the celebration. Here, soft knitted classics will take care of your needs. If the party is away from home, pack an extra outfit (or two) in the diaper bag just in case.

Keep your moses basket handy so baby can snooze in style and still be a part of this special occasion. Your "goo-ing and gaa-ing" guests will appreciate having the baby close by, too.

heirlooms

When Gracie was born I had no idea that she would actually use the silver rattle and spoon set that she received as a gift. By the time she was a year old, that rattle had many memorable dings in it — and she had already mastered her silver spoon. I am not one to collect things just to admire, so I was happy that these thoughtful gifts were already treasures, future heirlooms mined from these precious first years. When I found out that I was pregnant with Cecilia I wanted to find special pieces that could one day become her own heirlooms. She loves her silver rattle, too, and I'll never forget the first time that she held her silver brush to her head. She was so proud, Joe and I both ran for the camera. These items will make wonderful heirlooms because every dent and scratch holds special memories for all of us. Go ahead and use the beautiful things so they aren't simply objects in a curio cabinet, but become truly special and meaningful keepsakes.

I DESIGNED THIS SILK CHRISTENING GOWN AND BONNET FOR GRACIE, AND NOW THAT ALL OF OUR GIRLS WILL BE CHRISTENED IN IT, IT HAS BECOME A TRUE HEIRLOOM THAT CAN BE PASSED TO THE NEXT GENERATION. BRONZING YOUR BABY'S FIRST WALKING SHOES MAKES A CLASSIC KEEPSAKE THAT WILL ALWAYS HOLD SPECIAL MEMORIES.

collecting memories

After my babies were born, I was unbelievably tired, but I was on such a high — so in awe of the wondrous little person lying next to me — that it was the perfect opportunity to write down those amazing thoughts and feelings. When I read them now, I am instantly brought back to those precious moments. It never fails to bring tears to my eyes.

Here, I have designed my own photo albums and journals that hint at the story of the little life inside before you even open them. Children love to look at their baby pictures, to compare how much hair they had and how little they used to be. It's so much fun to peruse the albums together and experience that early joy all over again. Sharing scrapbooks and journals is a great way to get big brothers and sisters emotionally involved with the new sibling. This happy connection helps children appreciate and take pride in a new baby's milestones, strengthening the sibling bond.

celebrating the nest

Birds of a feather flock together, especially mama birds. As your family grows, so do the number of occasions you get to celebrate. Long before my life was blessed with children, I went above and beyond when it comes to parties. To me, celebrations are a time when its okay to go over the top, and that doesn't mean your budget has to. The extravagance should be in the details, which, if you know where to look and are willing to get crafty, can turn your party into an experience to be cherished forever. Isn't that what parties are all about?

baby showers

Every baby deserves to be showered with love. Whether it's your first or your fifth, by stork or surrogate, enjoy this special time to celebrate the new life you are bringing into the world.

FOR THIS COURTYARD BABY SHOWER I CHOSE A SOPHISTICATED BUT SWEET
STYLE THAT SAYS "IT'S A GIRL." THE TABLE, DECORATED WITH HAND-PAINTED
BIRDHOUSES, SETS THE STAGE FOR A BEAUTIFUL AND MEMORABLE DAY.

style and theme

If you are going to be involved in planning the festivities, think about what type of party you will enjoy most. Will it be a traditional tea with your closest girlfriends, a backyard extravaganza with family and friends, or an intimate couples dinner at your favorite restaurant? Also, think about the mood, whether you want your celebration to be sophisticated, elegant, cute or sweet. Then explore themes based on personal loves, hobbies — or even something that inspires you at the local craft store.

TO CREATE A SPECIAL CHAIR FOR THE GUEST OF
HONOR, I HAND-PAINTED A LITTLE SIGN THAT SAYS
"NESTING MAMA" AND ADDED SOME MOSS WITH A HOT
GLUE GUN. A VINE OF REAL TWIGS, EMBELLISHED
WITH RIBBONS AND A NEST, IS THE PERFECT RESTING
SPOT FOR THE PRECIOUS MAMA AND BABY BIRD.

A CLEVER KEEPSAKE:
THESE BIRDHOUSES
CAN LATER BE
WEIGHTED TO
MAKE BOOKENDS
FOR THE NURSERY.

THE BIRD'S NEST WREATH ON THE FRONT DOOR HINTS AT WHAT ONE
WILL FIND JUST INSIDE AND A HAND-PAINTED SIGN TELLS THAT THIS
CELEBRATION IS FOR BECKY. THE TOPIARY CENTERPIECE, DECORATED
WITH MINIATURE BIRDHOUSES AND BABY ROSES, IS SOMETHING
THAT THE GUEST OF HONOR CAN TAKE HOME AND NURTURE AS
AN EVER-GROWING MEMORY OF THE DAY.

For the baby shower pictured here, I chose a "nesting mama" theme because I fell in love with the unfinished birdhouses. I knew that I could paint them any way my imagination led me and the nesting theme was just so appropriate for a baby shower. Little did I know that the daddy-to-be was an ornithologist! Needless to say, when the guest of honor arrived she was overjoyed. And since she was 6000 miles away from her husband at the time, it made her feel close to him — making the party all the more special. When I suggested using some of the birdhouses for bookends or nightlights she was so excited that she decided to design her entire nursery around them.

"WISH FOR BABY" ENVELOPES WAIT TO BE PLUCKED BY EACH GUEST FROM A SWAG OF IVY GARLAND DRAPING OVER THE FIREPLACE.

AN ELEGANT CAKE TOPPED WITH A PINK ROSE AND
RASPBERRY FILLED CHAMPAGNE GLASSES WILL SOON BE
SAVORED BY GUESTS. ALTHOUGH YOU CAN'T PARTAKE IN
THE CHAMPAGNE, REMIND EVERYONE THAT PREGNANT
MOMMIES GET TO EAT AS MUCH CAKE AS THEY DESIRE!

gifts that keep on giving

Bows and boxes don't tell the whole story. It's easy and inexpensive to create this elegant world of mama and baby birds. You'll need craft supplies, a hot glue gun, and of course, your imagination.

All of these decorations — from the bird's nest door wreath with a personal greeting to the baby booty napkin rings — were so meaningful that the work became a labor of love. If you don't feel that you are creative or steady with a paintbrush, keep in mind that the beauty of paint is that you can fix any mistake with a wet paper towel and then start over. I painted the birdhouses freehand and added stenciling to the larger ones. It's fun to mix it up. The topiary tree was transformed into a beautiful centerpiece with the addition of miniature birdhouses and baby roses. The finishing touch was placing it in a simple clay pot (which I quickly whitewashed) and then wrapping the base with a ribbon.

To create a special chair for the guest of honor, I hand-painted a little sign that says "nesting mama" and added some moss with a hot glue gun. A vine of real twigs, embellished with ribbons and a nest, is the perfect resting spot for the precious mama and baby bird.

The most memorable details for everyone at this baby shower were the handmade "my wish for baby" envelopes and cards that I created to use with the birdhouse wish box. Each guest was invited to express in writing their own personal wish and dream for the baby. These notes were an exquisitely beautiful and intimate touch that mama and baby will treasure forever.

Another meaningful project was creating a special basket for party favors, like this one lined with moss to carry out the organic flavor of the party. Tucked between the beautiful packages was yet another style of miniature birdhouses, hand painted to add color and character in a way that highlights the sentimental theme.

My Wish for Baby

birthday parties

While some people spend days decking their house with Christmas lights and others construct elaborate haunted wonderlands for Halloween, the lion's share of my festive efforts go toward my little girls' birthdays. Planning a fabulous birthday can be as fun as enjoying the party. Here are some things to consider to make the day magical:

Personal theme What does the birthday child like? Consider favorite colors and interests. Gracie had two very particular requests for her second birthday ... to have "baby chickies" at her party and a lion cake that looked like one of her favorite stuffed animals.

Focus on the birthday child Don't let the little guest of honor get lost in the party. I made Gracie's pith helmet extra special for her by simply wrapping it with a band of leopard print fabric to coordinate with the cushion on her bamboo and palm throne. I also designed a special birthday safari dress that she still tries to squeeze into at three years old. It's so cute to watch this little explorer revisiting the memories of her party by searching a pretend jungle with her binoculars and pith helmet.

Entertainment Find entertainers with multiple skills, such as face painting, balloon animals, and maybe even magic tricks. Our safari entertainer came equipped with Gracie's wish of baby chickies.

Enjoy the party Enlist someone to help with food and guests so you can share this special time to eat cake with your baby — not just cut it.

THE SAFARI PROCESSIONAL, COMPLETE WITH A LEOPARD PRINT CUSHION AND REAL PALM FRONDS, WAS FASHIONED WITH DUCT TAPE AND A FEW LENGTHS OF BAMBOO FROM THE LOCAL GARDENING CENTER. AT CAKE-CUTTING TIME, GRACIE WAS THRILLED TO BE CARRIED IN LIKE A REAL SAFARI PRINCESS.

gracie's safari

Gracie loves animals, so I planned a backyard safari for her second birthday. The first thing I did was search catalogs and the Internet, where you can find amazing party accessories at an incredible value. We bought safari hats and play binoculars as favors so the children could find the inflatable animals hanging from the pint-sized jungle we created. To these little explorers, the few tall house plants placed opposite a row of hedges, combined with jungle sound effects (downloaded for free) could have been the Amazon itself. They loved it! And it warms my heart when, more than a year later, Gracie gets so excited when she visits friends and recognizes these cherished party favors from her safari!

gracie's grotto

Gracie loves mermaids, and months before her third birthday it became very clear to us that this was the theme she was wishing for. Since we'd been to many a great mermaid party in recent months, I thought I'd give Gracie's seaside soiree a bit of a different flavor. We would focus on the nuances of mermaid life.

With seaweed embellished invitations in the mail and a "small" grotto taking over my driveway, I got going on the finer details. In a mail-order party catalog, I found plastic shellfish, gold coins, strings of pearls, and shimmering curtains of silver and blue. It's always nice to present party favors in some sort of keepsake, so I found little paper boxes to paint and adorn with real seashells.

Instead of the usual party hats, Gracie's guests wore crab caps to explore the grotto and scoop up octopi, dolphins, and turtles from the sea pool. Afterwards, the children played pin the tail on the mermaid and dug into a treasure chest full of "gold" coins and sparkling "jewels."

One of Gracie's favorite touches was the illuminated fishbowls hanging from the cave walls. She thought it was so cool that there were real goldfish in there.

THIS MAGICAL MERMAID GROTTO WAS PLANNED WITH LIGHT-WEIGHT PVC PIPE, BUT ENDED UP BEING CONSTRUCTED FROM ENOUGH GALVANIZED PIPING TO PLUMB A BATHROOM! THE LABOR OF LOVE WAS WORTH THE EFFORT AS SOON AS WE SAW THE HUGE SMILE ON THE BIRTHDAY GIRL'S FACE.

cecilia's butterfly pavilion

When it came time for Cecilia's first birthday, we decided to have an intimate family gathering. In our family, that's still a significant number, so we moved the party outside for more space and put up a shady tent to avoid the hot sun. Butterfly has always been Cecilia's nickname, so we draped fabric beneath the tent to create a fanciful place for butterflies to rest. This also brought the ceiling level down to a more cozy level. Magical and functional!

Starting with the invitations, it was clear that this party was all about our little butterfly reaching a milestone. I included all of the things that she loves, like her favorite stuffed gray kitty as the birthday cake (adorned with edible flowers and butterflies that matched the invitation). Her high chair became a seat fit for a princess, with her name embroidered on the simple slipcover trimmed with a butterfly and a rose.

A transformed piñata served as a personal and oh-so-sweet centerpiece for the tent. To create this special accent, I simply removed all the shiny mylar and cartoon characters and replaced them with a beautiful photo of Cecilia surrounded by daisies and reindeer moss. The finishing touch was the organza ribbon hanging from each point. (Needless to say we did not actually use this as a piñata.)

At a craft store, I came upon daisy-themed wheelbarrows that would add to the garden party feel and make a perfect platform for presenting party favors. Here is a great example of how keeping an open eye and an open mind wherever you go can present opportunities for the unique elements that can really highlight the occasion. After all, who actually goes out looking specifically for a wooden, daisy-themed wheelbarrow?

For the favors themselves I found some heart-shaped, paper boxes that were already painted silver. All I did was add the same butterflies to the lids that were on the invitations. These boxes served as whimsical cocoons for the butterfly earrings picked especially for each little girl. Standard party blowers added to the wheelbarrow were customized to fit the occasion by adding a bow of ribbon and another butterfly.

BY SEEING BEYOND BASIC CORRESPONDENCE CARDS YOU CAN CREATE PERSONALIZED INVITATIONS THAT WILL SET THE TONE FOR THE SPECIAL DAY.

CECILIA'S CAKE RESEMBLES HER FAVORITE STUFFED GRAY KITTY, COMPLETE WITH EDIBLE FLOWERS AND BUTTERFLIES THAT MATCH THE INVITATIONS. HER HIGH CHAIR WAS TRANSFORMED INTO A SEAT FIT FOR A PRINCESS, WITH HER NAME EMBROIDERED ON THE SIMPLE SLIPCOVER TRIMMED WITH A BUTTERFLY AND A ROSE.

twig by twig

Birds don't build cozy nests overnight. Beyond collecting materials, they must devote themselves to the little ones until they can fly off on their own. In the same way, creating a nurturing home for your loved ones involves more than providing a beautiful environment. The heart of my philosophy lies in combining all of the elements that inspire a comforting home of intimacy and ease, a place for your family to bond and build beautiful memories together.

LAUGHTER AND TOUCH GET TO THE HEART OF BONDING.

bonding

People toss the word "bonding" around as if it's a handy tube of glue. The fact is, there are many ways to strengthen the love and respect between parent and child, and these vital elements provide the foundation of all you wish your child to be, the basis of your influence in helping your child grow to be a kind and caring person. This precious bond will develop between you, twig by twig.

When Cecilia was born, the nurse wanted to snatch her away to perform a newborn test. I refused to let her go, so they performed it right there on my bed. Then I learned why they wanted to take her away — have you ever seen how hard it is to squeeze a drop of blood from a newborn's heel? It's a tearful and heartbreaking proposition, but thank goodness I was there to comfort her. The point is, you have choices in your daily life that can make an enormous difference in your baby's comfort, security, and personal empowerment.

First, talk to your baby. All the time. About everything. Imagine what it would feel like to be carted around at will, without any explanation. Communication not only promotes language skills, but more importantly, it makes your baby secure. You are working towards building a mutual respect and trust from the very beginning. If you talk to your babies from day one they will know how important their feelings are. It's as simple as saying "Mama's going to pick you up," "here you go into the seat" and "I'm going to change your diaper now." I could go on and on, because I truly believe this is just as important as cuddling, hugging, and giggling together. Verbalize as much as possible and soon communication and consideration will come naturally to your child. It's even more gratifying when you realize that these qualities did not come naturally. They were learned from your example.

PLAY. PLAY. PLAY. Laughing with your child strengthens your bond — and it's just plain healthy. The more attention you give to your children, the more they are going to love and admire you. Our most meaningful playtime with the girls is at home. Every night after dinner we get silly and dance around our living room to a song called "By the Way" from the Red Hot Chili Peppers. The girls go nuts and we all crack up. "Again! Again! Again! — pleasieees." You know that saying "the best things in life are free?" You cannot buy the kind of joy this nightly ritual brings.

THE MOMENT YOUR BABY LOOKS INTO YOUR EYES FOR THE FIRST TIME IS
A MOMENT YOU WILL NEVER FORGET.

Getting down on the ground with your baby is also priceless. Don't stand on the sidelines and watch your little one play. Be the fun mom who climbs the slide and plays in the sand. I've had many a therapeutic tea party with my girls after a hard day at work. Climbing into their fort or building a castle in their sandbox allows me to get lost in their world — and focus just on them. When it comes to what's truly important, the little ones know best: having fun! And all the while, you are bonding and creating unforgettable memories.

WHEN GRACIE WAS A LITTLE BABY, ONE OF OUR FAVORITE THINGS TO DO WAS TO TAKE A TRANQUIL BATH TOGETHER. AS SHE GREW, BATH TIME TURNED INTO A MORE PLAYFUL TIME.

family time bonding

There's something about being naked together that inspires understanding and trust — the basic ingredients of bonding. When Gracie was a little baby I loved taking baths with her. It was a relaxing and tranquil experience. As she grew, it turned into more of a playful time together. And now, with the addition of Cecilia, I think I'd call them bath "parties." Still, it's another opportunity to focus on each other — all looking quite silly covered in bubbles and bath foam. This is also a special bonding time for the girls. Maybe it's the closeness of being stuck in the tub together, but they really share some amazing eye contact and laughs. They get silly splashing each other and Gracie gets a kick out of making bubble hairdos on her little sister.

just say yes

You can't *always* say yes, but use the word "no" sparingly. Negativity aside, opposing your child's will without fair and honest explanation will undermine your bond and diminish their self-confidence. However young they may be, always give your children the opportunity to understand — they will respect you for it and trust themselves to do the right thing next time. Positive reinforcement works better than anything else. It's also a far better way to go. One reason I like to design homes and nurseries that have bangable furniture and washable slipcovers is so that kids are free to be kids. It's much more fun to say yes.

When it comes to bigger questions, you can avoid saying "no" by taking an extra moment to be creative with your words. "Yes, you may have ice cream — after dinner." "Yes we can go outside and play — I'm so excited — but first you need to put your toys away." And, if they're still really little, add… "come on, let's do it together, Mama will help you." If you're consistent, positivity positively works.

GIVE THEM A TIMELINE Teaching Gracie the concept of "one minute, please," "first" and "after" has given her a very clear understanding (at a very young age) of what's expected. It has also taught her patience.

YOUR WORD IS YOUR BOND Good or bad, be it a reward or the loss of a privilege, never go back on your word. Never. There is nothing more valuable in any situation than the fact that if mommy or daddy says something, it is going to happen. (Of course, this does not include activities outside your control — flexibility is important there.) Your consistency gives them the kind of security that instills confidence and builds mutual respect. Adhering to this rule one-hundred-percent is among the hardest things to do in life, but when you commit to it, the rewards for you and your children are just as great.

do touch

While most everyone recommends baby-proofing your house, I like to think in terms of "house-proofing your baby." Of course it's important to put sharp objects and poison out of reach, to safeguard electrical outlets and swimming pools, but it's also important to teach your children how to interact with everything in your home. This is yet another aspect of bonding, because you are showing them that you trust them to learn and that they have the freedom to do so. This concept of "do touch" extends out into the real world on a daily basis.

The other day when I was at a home design store I heard an excited little boy exclaim, "Look at this. Can I hold it?" His mom simply said, "No, don't touch." I cringed at this response and wanted to run to him and say, "Of course you can hold it honey, but you need to be very gentle. Let me help you." The boy proceeded to pick up this object. Enter dad, "Your mother said 'don't touch.' Put that down." When the little boy asked why… "Because I said so, now put it back" — I had to leave that area of the store before I got myself into trouble. My point is, what kind of message are they sending to their child?

Moments like these (and they are plentiful) are the perfect opportunity to get down on your knees and show your child that you respect his feelings and have considered his request. By the time these parents were done arguing back and forth, they could have shared a special moment, taught their child a new skill, and built confidence at the same time.

You can start the process of "do touch" at home from the earliest moments of your child's exploration of their environment. Instead of packing up your breakables or labeling the living room "off limits," take the extra time to teach your baby the art of gentleness. Demonstrate how to interact with delicate items or certain areas. Of course, every baby has their own personality, so some may take longer than others to grasp the concept. Don't give up! If you are patient and consistent, they will get it and feel very proud.

During this process, keep in mind the importance of praise. Even when they're tiny and you are taking their hand to stroke something gently, clap and say "yay — good job!" Always make the praise a bigger deal than you think you should. Gracie picked up on the whole gentle and delicate thing very quickly, but Cecilia has taken more time. At fourteen months she still has her moments, but I know that our consistency and extra effort will soon pay off.

practical luxury

So many friends have come to our home and commented that no matter where you look, every angle is yummy and beautiful. They ask how everything stands up to young children and two big dogs. My answer: smart choices and slipcovers. Everywhere!

Building your decor, twig by twig, with practical luxury in mind is a helpful way to live out the vision of your children making tunnels from the living room sofa cushions and dancing around the piano, while you all share a beautiful evening fireside with good friends.

I like to decorate in family-friendly fabrics — washable, that is — so no matter who spills, everyone is comfortable. My furniture is heavy enough to withstand a toddler and finished with details that will blend right in with the inevitable nicks and scratches. If you can have hardwood floors in your home I highly recommend it. Footprints and paw prints, even the occasional spilled glass of milk, cause no worries. Smart décor choices from the very beginning translate to no "off limits" for your children and, more importantly, your children's comfort in every room of your home.

expanding the nest

Nesting birds are sheltered by nature, where the sky is the only limit to their dreams. While shelter is one of our basic necessities, we can enjoy the same freedom as our feathered friends by venturing out with our babies to explore the world together. Expand your nest into the great outdoors, where sunshine and cool grass between your toes add to the making of magical memories ... of that special place called home.

the great outdoors

One of the most refreshing things about children is how they are innately in tune with nature. I adore the fact that something as simple as a lemon tree or a little flower is so magical for Gracie and Cecilia. Every day they are full of wonder. They love digging in the dirt and collecting things from the garden. Pretty things and slimy things. Among their favorites: roly-polys.

Whether your yard is a sprawling expanse of nature or a rooftop garden in the city, you can make the most of your home by creating a view from each window that beckons your children to "come out and play." My basic rule of thumb is: when in doubt — plant. Block walls call for climbing vines like our "creeping fig."

A common walkway becomes an enchanted path when you line it with flowers. Whenever you can, involve your children in special gardening projects. This encourages their nurturing side and will help them to understand and appreciate the changing seasons.

FOR CHILDREN, THE SMALLER AND MORE PLANTED AN OUTDOOR AREA, THE BETTER IT IS FOR IMAGINATIVE PLAY. WE USE THIS SHADY DINING NOOK ON A DAILY BASIS FOR EITHER BREAKFAST, LUNCH OR DINNER. THE GIRLS LOVE EATING OUTDOORS AS MUCH AS WE DO AND WHEN THEY'RE FINISHED, THEY CAN RUN AND PLAY WHILE WE CATCH A MOMENT TO RELAX.

I SIMPLY ADORE THE FACT THAT SOMETHING AS SIMPLE AS A LEMON TREE
OR A LITTLE FLOWER IS SO MAGICAL FOR GRACIE AND CECILIA.

magical outdoor play places

My friend teases that if aliens take over the earth a millennium from now, they'll take one look at the plastic toddler furniture that survived and get the impression that humans were a race of very small people. While I'm all for practicality and extended use, peeking "outside of the box" of mainstream choices will enhance your yard and make it a truly magical place. From an old-fashioned tree swing to a cozy stone fireplace, I've added touches to our yard that have made it a friendly extension of our home. It's not only a place to run, jump, and climb, but also a place to explore, imagine, and create.

Transforming your yard into an outdoor sanctuary for both children and adults can be fun. Here's an opportunity to be creative and invent your own play places. When Gracie started playing with sand toys, I studied our yard to figure out a way to avoid the popular plastic turtle. Now we have a beautiful sandbox tucked into a corner of our yard — a project I put together with redwood planks, picket fencing, and wire. Everyone loves to join in and play in the sand under the shady canopy of flowering vines.

THIS TREE SWING HOLDS SO MANY MEMORIES FOR US, FROM ITS COMICAL BEGINNINGS WHEN MY UNCLE AND HUSBAND PUT IT UP, TO SWINGING ON IT FOR THE FIRST TIME WITH GRACIE WHEN SHE WAS ONLY FIVE DAYS OLD, TO SEEING WHAT A BIG GIRL SHE IS NOW, GOING ON IT ALL BY HERSELF. EVERY DAY SHE REQUESTS A TREE-SWING RIDE AND SHOUTS "HIGHER! HIGHER!"

THERE'S NOTHING LIKE RELAXING UNDER THE STARS WITH A MARSHMALLOW ROAST. OUR BACKYARD FIREPLACE IS A YEAR-ROUND FAMILY GATHERING PLACE. TUCKED INTO A ROMANTIC LITTLE CORNER, THIS SPOT IS ENJOYED BY EVERYONE IN THE FAMILY — AND WHEN MARSHMALLOWS ARE INVOLVED, THAT INCLUDES OUR DOGS, GATSBY AND GRISWALD. IF YOU AREN'T READY FOR A STONE FIREPLACE, A SMALL CHIMNEY FROM A GARDEN CENTER WILL DO NICELY.

A STORYBOOK STONE PATH LEADS AROUND THE
PLAY GYM TO A HOMEMADE SANDBOX SHADED BY
A CANOPY OF FLOWERING VINES. COMPLETE WITH
KID-LEVEL PLAY TABLES AND A WATER STATION,
THIS LITTLE AREA OF OUR YARD SPARKS THE
IMAGINATION AND INSPIRES CREATIVITY.
OUTDOOR PLAY PLACES THAT ARE SPECIFIC TO
CHILDREN PROMPT ADVENTUROUS OUTDOOR
LUNCHES. THIS STURDY TABLE IS ALSO IDEAL FOR
FINGER PAINTING AND OTHER MESSY PROJECTS.

YOU CAN CREATE A MAGICAL OUTDOOR PLAY PLACE JUST BY SPREADING A BLANKET ON THE LAWN AND HAVING A TEA PARTY. IT'S THE TOGETHERNESS THAT PROVIDES THE MAGIC. AND IT'S SO EASY TO PULL OUT PLAY TUNNELS AND PARACHUTES TO HAVE YOUR OWN PRIVATE MOMMY-AND-ME (OR DADDY-AND-ME) SESSION. THEN AGAIN, OLD FASHIONED TUMMY TICKLING CAN BE JUST AS FUN!

THIS FOUNTAIN, WHICH IS EASY AS 1-2-3 TO INSTALL, MAKES A BEAUTIFUL VISUAL STATEMENT AND IS AN INSTANT WATER-PLAY AREA. FLOWERS PLUCKED FROM OUR GARDEN DOUBLE AS MAGICAL CUPS AND MINIATURE RAFTS. WE EVEN HIDE A STASH OF PENNIES NEARBY FOR MAKING WISHES. OF COURSE, WE ALWAYS SUPERVISE THE CHILDREN AROUND WATER — WITH AN ENVIRONMENT THIS BEAUTIFUL, IT'S A PLEASURE TO SIMPLY SIT AND WATCH.

dvd contents

NURSERY DESIGN Wendy Bellissimo

PARTY DESIGN Wendy Bellissimo

WRITTEN WITH Leslie Lehr Spirson

ART DIRECTOR AND DESIGNER
Kristin Holloway NVU PRODUCTIONS

VIDEO EDITOR AND DVD AUTHOR
Michael Lister NVU PRODUCTIONS

BOOK AND DVD PRODUCTION NVU Productions

PRESIDENT Jim Forni

CHIEF CREATIVE OFFICER Tom O'Grady

PRODUCER Liz Fulton

PRODUCTION MANAGER Melinda Fry

Karen Keenan, Sue Young, Tim Sheridan, Joe Ranieri

John Fuller, Andrew Falconer

credits & thanks

PHOTOGRAPHY

Image Arts, Inc. in Woodland Hills, CA. PAGES 86, 96–97

Cameron Carothers PAGES 26–27, 30–33, 38–39, 46–47

Delbert Garcia PAGES 52–55, 58–59

Evan Sklar PAGES 34–37, 66–67

Handleand Tesoro PAGES X–1, 2–11, 68–69, 86, 88–95, 106–108, 113–114, 116, 118, 125, 134

John Payne PAGES 75–85

Katrine Naleid PAGES 98–101

Larsen and Talbert PAGES 13–17, 20–25, 28–29, 40–45, 48–55, 60–65, 70–73, 102–105, 107–112, 114–115, 117–124, 126–133

Lisa Romerin PAGES 56–57

Paul Wicheloe PAGES 18–19

MAKEUP Rosemary Redlin

STYLING Karlee Artist Management

WARDROBE Cary Robinson

HAIR Daniel Abriol

VIDEOGRAPHY Revolver Films

DIRECTOR OF PHOTOGRAPHY Matt Mindlin

AUDIO MIXER Erik Simulcik

UTILITY Derek Lynch

DIGITAL PREPRESS Resource Graphic, Inc.

PRINTER Mondadori Printing

//PERSONAL THANKS//

Thanks to my husband, who encouraged me to sell my first creation and never let me give up; to my mom, my Aunt Francine, and my Uncle John, who trusted in me and gave me my first loan when no bank would; to Freddie & Daisy, my grandparents, who set the example that hard work pays off; and to Auntie Gail, who always took care of us during those grueling New York trade shows. Special thanks to Paul Spadone for the introduction, to Al Hassas, who believed in my talent, and to Jim, Liz, Kristin, and Mike at NVU: I am so grateful for your vision and dedication to this book and for helping to make it a reality. To Jen, for your creativity and help with those late night projects, and to Maria, for sticking with us from our earliest beginnings. To everyone at Wendy Bellissimo baby 'n' kids, who always help to make things happen. To Leslie Spirson, who understands a mother's love and need to be with her children at every moment possible: thank you for your wit and talent and for helping to make this all happen wherever (Labor & Delivery) and whenever (at two in the morning) possible. To the parents who welcomed me into their homes to be a part of such an exciting and special time: thanks for the memories that each of you have given me and for making my work feel so meaningful. Finally, to my children, outside and inside my tummy: if it were not for you and how you teach and inspire me every day, this book would not exist.

//THANKS TO//

101 FLOWERS, WOODLAND HILLS, CALIFORNIA for your beautiful work with the baby shower flowers.

PENNY ERLICH for making my vision of dreamy murals a reality.

KIM SHEA for your help with Fun With Paints.

MARCO FRANCHINA for the lovely journal photography.

MIA BOUDREAU for sharing your home for a very special baby shower and for sharing BABY MILA, our bathing beauty.

FLORA AND HENRI for the beautiful baby clothes.

//SPECIAL THANKS TO//

FABI AND MARIA for the love and comfort that you always give to our girls; your dedication and care are treasured by all of us, every day. We love you.

DANIELA, OUR ANGEL SENT FROM ITALIA, you saved us. We love and miss you.

BETH, OUR NEIGHBOR AND FRIEND, you are truly special and we love you. Thanks for all your help.

FOR FURTHER INFORMATION OR RESOURCES PLEASE VISIT:
WWW.NESTING.COM
OR WWW.WENDYBELLISSIMO.COM